T0209784

The Beauty
Of
God's Goodness
&
Faithfulness

A succinct Autobiography
of
Suffering to Surrendering to Jesus Christ

DOR MAE FORBES

authorHOUSE®

AuthorHouse™
1663 Liberty Drive
Bloomington, IN 47403
www.authorhouse.com
Phone: 1 (800) 839-8640

Published by AuthorHouse 10/17/2019

ISBN: 978-1-7283-3219-2 (sc)
ISBN: 978-1-7283-3218-5 (e)

Print information available on the last page.

Any people depicted in stock imagery provided by Getty Images are models, and such images are being used for illustrative purposes only. Certain stock imagery © Getty Images.

Scripture quotations marked KJV are from the Holy Bible, King James Version (Authorized Version). First published in 1611. Quoted from the KJV Classic Reference Bible, Copyright © 1983 by The Zondervan Corporation.

Scripture quotations marked NIV are taken from the Holy Bible, New International Version®. NIV®. Copyright © 1973, 1978, 1984 by International Bible Society. Used by permission of Zondervan. All rights reserved. [Biblica]

Scripture quotations marked NKJV are taken from the New King James Version. Copyright © 1982 by Thomas Nelson, Inc. Used by permission. All rights reserved.

This book is printed on acid-free paper.

CONTENTS

My Cup Runneth Over With Thanks!

Heavenly Father:

Giving honor, glory and praise to the One True God, who is my Heavenly Father, Jesus Christ my personal Savior and the powerful indwelling of the Holy Spirit. The ***goodness and faithfulness of God*** I have surely experienced over the years ever since I was in my mother's womb until now and I am confident of this that I will continue to receive. Truly God exists! I am grateful that I have been ***gracefully broken*** by His loving Hands and Heart that kept me through the different seasons of my life. Thank you Lord for never leaving me or forsaking me. You are my constant. I know you as my Father and I know you as a Friend who sticks closer than a brother. You have always provided and protected me. Your presence and power have strengthened me through.

I love you forever my Lord and King.

~~~~~~~~

To the loves of my life:

Dearest Mama Joy: You are my day one tower
of strength, love, support, wisdom, confidant
and joy. Thank you for believing in me, for
building me up, for pushing me forward
and showing me how to labor to the end.
Dearest Daddy Intellectual: You have
graduated from this earth but you are alive
in my consciousness. I am proud to be fabric
from your being, the physical continuation
of the power of the pen and the voice
that will herald God's word. Amen.
My wonderful Brother Encourager: You are my
extra shoulder to lean on and voice of reason
I can depend on. Thanks for your guidance
and strong support throughout the years

which have made a marked difference in my life. God gave me His best to be my brother. My powerful son King: You are the beat of my heart and the joy running through my veins. Thanks for being the wind beneath my wings, tissue for my tears and one reason why I smile this wide.

~~~

Thanks to all my family, friends, spiritual mentors and leaders: I am grateful for your presence in my life. I cannot thank you all enough!

Goodness of God

Song by Bethel Music and Jenn Johnson

(an excerpt)

I love You Lord

For Your mercy never failed me

All my days, I've been held Your hands

From the moment that I wake up

Until I lay my head

Oh, I will sing of the goodness of God

PREFACE

It was May 2019 when the idea of this book was seeded in my Spirit while having a conversation with a fellow co worker. I actually wanted to write my autobiography for many years seeing that I have much to share, however, I delayed year after year until that said day in May.

I have always enjoyed speaking with this specific co worker. She shared lots about her life and I reciprocated. She had experience and knowledge that I believe God wanted her to share with me. Time spent with her was never wasted. Revelations ebbed and flowed as we conversed with each other. Of course, this was often to our benefit as we both listened and grew. I thank God for her because she was the vessel that God used to bridge me to my NEXT!

That day, we happened to talk about a flurry of topics namely: favor, trust, relationships and truth. I advised her to start writing and that's when she revealed that she had volumes of poems which she compiled over the years since childhood. I told her: "Publish them!" She chuckled and that's when the BIG IDEA launched out my gut. That BIG IDEA launched me to do a compilation of autobiographical events of my life. And hence I was propelled again unto the great highway of writing. The pen in my hand flowed ink like a river on paper. I was swimming in my element again like a fish in water.

This book is a compilation of testimonies of my life that shows the goodness and faithfulness of God. I am evidence that God is good and will do great things in your life if only you allow Him to. This book tells of the power and mercy of God's hand channeling my life from struggling with issues to surrender to the leadership of the Holy Spirit. It is a history book of how God took my messes and mistakes and birthed relevant messages and successful missions. My life has been an elixir of joys, frustrations, inner battles, outer frictions, batters of painful lessons which all churned together for my good. I am an example of what the POTTER does when the clay surrenders. He indeed turns the clay into a beautiful masterpiece.

Surely, I have learned that all things work together for our good, even when we don't understand what's happening and it may seem unfair or unclear. God can and will use what you have endured for your good and His glory.

Birthing this evangelistic autobiography (a term I created), was not the smoothest process. It is the first time I am writing under a PEN NAME which is DOR MAE FORBES. I cried many times birthing this book. I struggled to expose some secret areas of my life. It was a laborious process birthing this book with facing all types of issues popping up unexpectedly, but I had to press forth to do what God has called me to do for Him. I am confident of this, that this book will bless you and teach you in some way, if not many ways.

My life has had many uprisings and downsizings, but I still stand strong in my Savior and Lord Jesus Christ, continually being led by the Holy Spirit of God and praying fervently, praising unashamed and putting my faith in the One who created me for His good pleasure. You will find that a scripture accompanies each chapter as I share some of the challenges and joys I experienced since teenage years to middle age. Despite all the issues I faced, I can now say today that I love the woman I have become and I love my life because my perspectives shift when I face challenges. God allows us to face challenges because He knows we have been equipped to handle them. We simply need to develop that underdeveloped muscle and become stronger still. Where I used to complain about issues, I now ask God: "Speak to me Lord. Teach me you way. What do you want me to know, learn or unlearn?"

God has truly been good to me. He has showed up when I was on my last thread of hope and at my worst feelings of desperation. God has blocked the plans of the enemy to destroy my life, future and destiny. The Holy Spirit has been and still is my Advocate when others shut doors in my face and speak evil of me. God's mercy kept me from falling and my life from failing. His love lavitated me out of the lion's lunges and He has kept faithful to His Word for my life. I see all His promises manifesting in my life for His glory. I pray you will see a sliver of yourself somewhere in my journey, because at the end of the day I have realized that we aren't that different from each other. May hope rise up in you to know that it isn't over for you! God has the final say in your life. Repeat that! God has the final say over my life!! In Jesus name Amen!

Allow me to share a personal encounter I had a few years ago.

One night I had a vision and I heard a verse of a song that rang true to my heart and my life. In the vision I was singing and these are the words I heard:

"Oh how Great is our God! I finally get to see what your commitment means to me."

I am not sure if such a song exists with these same words, but all I know for sure is this: God has truly been faithful and true to me even through the storms and tests. He has never failed me and I know that all the things I have faced was for my good so others can believe that He is real and all glory belongs to Him. **I, Dor Mae Forbes (pen name), do believe that you will be blessed, encouraged and transformed by my story... because God made me to be one out of His many lights to shine brightly His glory in this world. God bless you and be encouraged through my journey in Jesus name Amen!**

Coming to America

~Escaping the Pain of Heartbreak~

Romans 8:28 KJV "And we know that
***all things work together for good t*o
them** that love God, to them who are
called according to ***His purpose*.*"*

I was 16 years old when I faced my first heartbreak. As a teen I was very outgoing, brash and opinionated. I had a mouth that held nothing back and I in essence kept it real with my friends, family and people I came into contact with. I am the same to be frank, but I am learning each

1

day to do all that I do from the framework and foundation of love. We can be direct and speak our truth from the place of love.

During my teen years, I was part of a group called the St. Patrick's crew. Most of the girls in the group were in a relationship with guys in the group. We did a lot together from going to different fetes, studying and restauranting. My boyfriend's name was Mitch and we were tight and alright. We were inseparable and constantly with each other on the weekends. He, being a pastor's son, was quite a talker and very astute in the Word of God. Needless to say, I wasn't a Christian then, but God surely was using him as a vessel to seed my life with the Word of God. As Mitch beheaded chickens in his parents spacious backyard and preached to me at the same time, he was very protective and mindful of guarding my sight from seeing the gory and brutal ways he ended the lives of the chickens. I admired him for that because seeing blood was something I feared seeing. Although Mitch and I were teens, we had a genuine affinity and respect for each other until he decided to end the relationship... abruptly.

The day Mitch ended the relationship was the day my life took on a different trajectory. That day we almost had sex for the first time. We had agreed to meet after my last examinations at his house. Everything was set. His parents and siblings weren't home. He had the room and mood ready and at 16, I thought I was ready. We were both in birthsuit form when it seemed as if something struck him as he stood armored in front of me. The next thing I knew, he was commanding me to put my clothes on. Nothing happened and I was totally confused. The heat of the moment was quenched by his commands to get dressed.

As he walked me down the long rocky road towards my house, he gave me a drilling as if we were in trouble. I never forgot the words.

"I will be a doctor and nothing will stop me. I can't see you any longer."

My heart was smashed to pieces. My best friend was telling me that we were over. I didn't know how to process it and so I internalize the anger. I carried the fissure in my heart, mind and soul for several years. Other relationships I had somehow didn't work and compounded into more heartbreak. That initial breakup was the template that set the stage for other breakups because I didn't get closure prior to leaving Jamaica and coming to America. I was crushed to the point I couldn't function properly at school and so I sought an escape route. I planned to come to America to spend the summer with my first cousin Marshall, and unbeknownst to my parents, I had no intent to return. The reason I wanted to escape was because I had difficulty facing the pain of seeing Mitch when I was around my peers. I could tell he was hurting as much as I was. I decided to run… to a different land.

My plan of coming to America was successful until my life started shifting suddenly. In retrospect, I witnessed how the beauty of God's Hands worked in my life. God strategically used a painful breakup to get me to America because He had a plan for me here. The enemy fought me long and hard in my emotions to give up, but God made sure to it I remained strong and maintained my integrity and dignity. Being in America was not the smoothest ride for me. I encountered blatant racism, classism, divorces, jealousy, hatred, abuse, discrimination, lied on, lied to, being partially homeless, jobless, rejected, mishandled, raped and so much more. Despite these toxic experiences, I never lost faith that things would get better. I learned new lessons and unlearned obsolete and erroneous teachings.

Fleeing to America because I didn't want to face the pain of heartbreak placed me in a triathlon. I was spiritually swimming, cycling and running through life. I swam through the deep scary waters of two divorces and being a single parent. I cycled up high and steep obstacles of living from house to house, jealousy on the job and in ministry and ran through dark valleys of despair dealing with being jobless. I have eaten bread and water of sorrows and partook in hefty joyous feasts. I sowed in tears, yet reaped in joy. I understand now that I had to be processed for purpose. God is still processing for His purposes. God had to reveal to me that I have to become His ultimate vision: His woman of character.

It took me about 20 years to finally let go of the fragments of that heartbreak which occured at the tender age of 16. Although I got saved years after the heartbreak, I didn't realize that I wasn't delivered from that pain. It took one apology from Mitch and a prayer to God to please settle my heart. We reconnected via a mutual friend who explained that Mitch had often queried about me. I had visited her in Barbados one year and Mitch and I reconnected via Facebook. He apologized and explained that at the time he was studying for the entrance exam for the university he wanted to attend, he couldn't focus because all he saw on the pages of the book was my face. I was a distraction to him and so the best route for him was to end the relationship. I hadn't known this, but was grateful for the explanation. It made a world of difference. I was able to move on from there and press forward to do bigger and better things like writing this, my sixth book.

I pray that you understand that everything that we face has a purpose. God in His Omniscience is molding us even through negative experiences. He sees us in the future and there are certain characteristics in us that need His attention and His mighty Hand of healing. We need to learn to forgive, grant mercy and to love again. God wants us to be His masterpieces to reflect His glory. We cannot allow the pain of heartbreak to seize us from becoming. We are to learn to face the pain of heartbreak. We too break the Heart of the Father. His heart breaks when we are not in alignment with His will. His heart breaks when we choose to live life without Him. His heart breaks when we reject His instructions. We break the heart of God when we place idols in view and worship them, instead of worshipping Him.

Sometimes we have to feel what heartbreak is, to understand how God feels when we break His heart.

Let us refuse to run away from what God wants us to face. It is in facing the pain we become stronger. God is building us in the midst of the pain and we will develop the stamina to go further. You will never face it alone once you invite the Lord in the midst of it all. Amen.

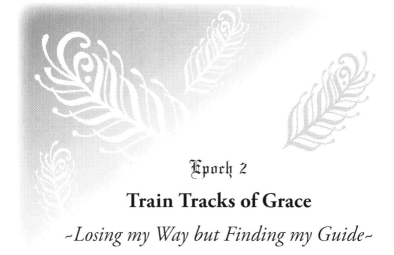

Epoch 2

Train Tracks of Grace

~Losing my Way but Finding my Guide~

2 Corinthians 12:9 NIV

"My grace is sufficient for you, for my
power is made perfect in weakness."

My strategic plan of escaping the pain of
heartbreak was to come to America to spend the
summer with my first cousin Marshall. What
no one knew was: I wasn't planning to return to
Jamaica.

I finished my first year of lower 6 in Jamaica,
which is pre-college studies. I couldn't focus and

hence I failed most of my classes. I had lost all interest in studying and I know now it was in correlation to the broken condition of my heart. I felt like my heart was in a million pieces. My aim to skip town and start life over in America was at the forefront in my mind and nothing was going to stop me.

That summer with my cousin and his girlfriend in the States was very good, but they needed to get back to their normal lives. My dad who normally visited the states as well, was surprised when I told him I didn't want to go back to Jamaica. I somehow convinced him that I wanted to go to college in the states rather than Jamaica. He, knowing lots of people, contacted one of his friends, Ms. Lewis, who lived in New Jersey. He made arrangements with her to provide housing and sponsorship in exchange for a monthly payment that would cover tuition, housing and food. So, before my dad returned to Jamaica he moved me to live with Ms. Lewis in New Jersey.

At first, things seemed to be working living with Ms. Lewis, until she decided she wanted to be an opportunist of the arrangement. She cleverly incorporated making me her personal assistant and house servant. She expected me to cook, clean, do laundry, and run her banking and laundry errands. When she realized that I wasn't the type to be bossed around, she executed a plan for my demise.

Ms. Lewis had a teenage son who lived with her and gave her more trouble than a hurricane. Although he and I were around the same age, his anger proved he had some serious issues. The turbulent relationship he had with his mother was evidenced by the strong tension that I often felt in the home when he decided to be there. We didn't speak often, but when we did it was quite brief. I pitied him because he was a brewing storm ready to cause destruction. Ms. Lewis often visited Jamaica and so she decided that autumn, she was going to leave me in the house alone with her son. Hardly any food was in the house and I had no money.

The day she flew to Jamaica was the same day my mother had planned to give Ms. Lewis and myself an unannounced visit. They happened to see each other at the airport and my mother was less than happy to learn she had left me in the house alone with her son. Needless to say, my mother was livid. My mother immediately had my brother call the house and instructed me to remain in the hallway until she got there. As I reminisce of this event, I witness the goodness of God's Hand at work on my behalf guarding me. That evening as it got dark, Ms. Lewis' son walked into the house with four of his husky friends whom I had never seen before. My nerves and inner alarms went on high alert and immediately I got out of the apartment and went for a very long walk. When I returned, I stayed in the hallway for over 6 hours. Her son would pop his head out to ask if I wasn't going to bed and of course my answer was a stern and abrupt "NO". I sensed that they were waiting for me out to get tired but I held out. Relief came to my heart when my mother arrived at 4 am the following morning. As she entered the apartment, the husky teens were shocked to see my Mom and they all left immediately.

You see, what the enemy had planned, God prevented. This is one of the wonders of God's Hand at work in our lives. My mother explained that she had flown to JFK with the intent to stay by her nephew in Brooklyn and travel to New Jersey in the morning. When she saw Ms. Lewis at the airport, she sensed I was in danger and quickly shifted plans and made her way straight from the airport to New Jersey. That trip from JFK was a miracle because according to my mom, there was a man with a van picking up people at the airport and taking them to New Jersey. This man, after making several drop offs, took my mother to her destination.

How protective is our God? Very! He will cause the heavens and the earth to move to protect His Beloved Ones. If God went to the extent to have His Only Begotten Son Jesus die for us, then what else would He not do for us? God sees way into our future and intentionally makes ways for us. He provides all that a person needs and He will block the intentions of the enemy. I have often witnessed the extent of God's love through the heart of my parents. My mother especially has an enormously giving heart that keeps on giving to her children, the church and others, even strangers. I am so grateful that God has blessed my life with such an amazing and loving mom. She has made massive sacrifices for us and I don't have enough words to thank her. So, with ink on paper, I thank the God who created my dear mother just for me. She has been a grand backbone and fierce fighter for our survival.

My time being at Ms. Lewis' house was short lived after that incident. My parents had a serious talk with her and so minimal adjustments were made. I wasn't happy being in her house anymore because I sensed an ominous presence with her. There are some people you can sense their feelings about you without them even saying a word. I wanted to leave her house so badly, I prayed long and hard. The day came when she told me I had to leave and return to New York to my cousin. I spoke with my cousin and he suggested

I return to Jamaica, but that was a no-no for me. I remember the night I prayed that the Lord would make a way for me. I prayed it seemed the entire night till 6am the morning. I prayed and cried to God asking Him for a way out. There was a train that ran behind the house and as it roughed the tracks and rackled my bed and contents in my room, and so I was comforted feeling rocked in the arms of God. I somehow knew in my heart that all would be well. I continued my classes at the community college I was attending. I excelled in all my classes and boasted my grades to Ms. Lewis who wasn't impressed at all. Her behaviour pushed me further away from her, but God was brewing up some goodness for me again. That goodness was revealed on a public bus ride home from college. I was heavily concerned about how I would be delivered from Ms. Lewis.

The manifestation of God's goodness and faithfulness occured as I rode on the bus home from college. I met a young lady who happened to be Jamaican. Her name: Jazzy. Jazzy was quite energetic and friendly. She kept chatting and chatting asking me a ton load of questions as I tried to ignore her loud and brash behavior. My mind was consumed with my situation and the last thing I wanted was a Q&A session.

Jazzy decided to work my nerves with chatter until she asked me a question that jolted my attention.

Jazzy: "Why do you look like you have the world on your shoulders? The world isn't coming to an end, you know. Smile nuh?"

Me: "I have a situation."

Jazzy: "You remind me of my best friend in Jamaica. You look like Debbie with your pretty and cute face!"

I wasn't excited by, nor interested in her compliments and she continued to bother me with questions.

Jazzy: "So what's your problem? Maybe I can help you."

After explaining to her my dilemma, she somehow cajoled me to go home with her to meet her grandmother. Me not knowing her, nor her grandmother took a step of faith and followed her home. Somehow I trusted her and after speaking with her grandmother, who fell in love with me immediately, sat me down and explained in her humble and sweet voice that she was willing to help me. I remember her words:

"I don't have much to offer you but food and shelter. You can sleep in the living room. It gets very cold in there during the winter, but I will give you heaters to help you stay warm"

I trusted Grandma. Something about her made me trust her immediately and I agreed to go and stay with them. Jazzy was super excited and I could see the visible excitement in her eyes.

Again, this was another display of the goodness and faithfulness of God working in my life. He answered my prayers in such a way that brought such peace to the turmoil I was facing. God arranged it for me to meet and speak with Jazzy on a bus. God was bussing me to my next nest! Jazzy was taken aback by my resemblance of her best friend in high school in Jamaica and she was authentically concerned about my visibly worried facial expression. She was moved to help me and it worked out for my good. Isn't God an amazing Father? You see, God is always at work in our lives. We may not recognize it immediately, but God is always willing to step into our situations if we invite Him. It's all but a prayer away and then we have to wait on Him to lead us to the solution or the solution to us.

I moved out of Ms. Lewis' house not long after. She was away at work when I did so. She had two daughters who were older than I was. I was closer to the youngest one who also had issues with her mother. I had confided in her my intentions of leaving and she invited me to spend a weekend with her prior to moving. On my way home after the weekend visit, I had an unusual encounter. I took the train, got off the correct station, but did not exit properly. As I walked and walked, I got confused with my directions and somehow ended up on train tracks which I thought were no longer in use. The reason I thought the tracks were no longer in use was because there was also another Caucasian woman walking on the track and she had a huge black bag on her shoulders. Although she kept her distance, I somehow got a chance to acknowledge her with a hello, and inquired whether or not I was going in the right direction when I told her the address. She nodded her head and smiled but kept walking behind me. One thing I particularly noticed about her was her eyes. They were the brightest blue I had seen. Her eyes seemed to glow and it was as if I was looking at the sky. I asked her again if I was closer because it seemed as if I was walking forever. I knew I was walking alongside a road because I could hear cars and see the traffic lights. It was beginning to get dark and so I felt it necessary to get off the train tracks. The woman by this time was walking a bit ahead of me and she turned and motioned to me to climb up the slope to the street. She never said a word. All she did was pointed towards the street level. As I struggled up the slope maneuvering through bushes and shrubs, I heard a train horn in the distance. I was puzzled. As I got to street level, I was able to figure out my location. It wasn't even five minutes after making it to street level, I heard the train horn again blowing loudly and the familiar tethering and tottering of the train speeding and riding the tracks I just got off. My heart leapt. I was speechless. God had spared my life from what could have been a fatality. God got me off the tracks at the right time even though I had lost my way. God provided a guide and showed me grace just in time. How great is our God? His grace and his goodness is sufficient for me.

That has been the story of my life. I have often lost my way and metaphorically gotten myself on dangerous tracks, but God always sent the right guides to help me get back on the right path. God has often extended his Hand of grace pointing me back on the right roads that I must take instead of remaining in harm's way. I am thankful that

I have been spared time and again all because of His grace and mercy.

God's goodness showed up via my Mom's quick thinking and surprise visit to New Jersey. God's faithfulness showed up through meeting Jazzy on the bus. God used Grandma to assist me from returning home, by opening her home and receiving me to live with her. And God showed up by allowing that caucasian woman with the sky blue eyes to get me off the train tracks just in time. I am especially thankful to Grandma who opened her doors to meet my needs. Grandma fed me and loved me as her own. Jazzy and I had a great relationship for that season and we loved and grew together.

My mother went back home and settled some business before returning to America to be with me. Her presence with me in America made a difference and I have learned that family is really

important when you are in a strange land. The Lord has been good to me and has shown me kindness in several ways. I encourage you to take the time to see His Hand of Divine Goodness and Faithfulness in your life. Believe me, God will allow us to audit our lives so that we can recognize that He was and still is our ever present help in times of trouble.

Epoch 3

Pennies in a Pond

*~Wishes do Come True but
Sometimes Turn Blue~*

3 John 1:2 KJV

"Beloved, I wish above all things

that you prosper and be in health,

even as your soul prospers."

Living with Grandma was what I needed at that time and I knew that it was God who arranged the relationship. She was deeply grateful for the financial help from my parents and I needed the downtime and the change of environment.

Although Grandma died several years after I left New Jersey, the last time I visited her after not seeing her for over five years, she said to me: "I can die now." I told her not to say those words but she meant them. It was less than a year after I saw her, she did pass away and I wept. Even now writing this, I cried.

God has a way of showing us that none of us are random beings. Grandma served her purpose on earth as a woman of God who was a devout Seventh Day Adventist. She loved her children and grandchildren and all those she helped. I am grateful that her life made a difference in mine. She could have turned her back on me, but she didn't. She knew God had sent me to her care, and she cared for me well, feeding, praying, and loving me. Thank you Lord for Grandma. Thank you Lord for your love through this woman of God. I look forward to seeing her in heaven and that smile that warmed my heart. Her life, as well as, my mother's example of caring for others have molded me. We aren't here for our own selfish needs. God desires that we help others. The more we help others, the more God helps us. Let us endeavour to be a blessing to others by helping them.

Jazzy and I had a blast living together in New Jersey. She had a little bully side to her, always wanting to try the most outlandish adventures and I was her partner following the craziness at times. Despite her carefree ways, God knew that I was her voice of reason and balance. There were times I would forcefully let her know I wasn't going to join in on some of her craziness and because she needed a partner to do her shenanigans, she would simply back down when I resisted. I have realized that God knows who to place in our lives at the right time for the right purposes. He loves us so much he knows who to send to show us the way and bring us some sort of balance and temperance. Jazzy and I were both firecrackers, but there were times we both needed to become water for each other. My stay at the house in New Jersey with them wasn't perfect, but I was safe. I was able to secure a job and of course invited Jazzy to join me. We both dropped out of college but we excelled quickly on our job, but I had to leave because my life took another sudden shift.

As I think back, I remember what caused the shift. It was a penny in a pond "wish", but now I know it was a prayer. I was off from work that day and I frequently visited a mall that had an outdoor water fountain that people would throw coins in and cast wishes into. The fountain base had lots of pennies. That day, I was sad. I had a lot on my mind because I felt like I was stuck and I needed a change of pace. There were certain aspirations

I had at the time. I wanted to return to college, get a better job, get married, have children, get a home and a car. I had many aspirations, but I had limitations. I didn't have certain necessities to accomplish these goals. Without them I was at a standstill. Grandma knew my predicament and had informed me that getting married would change my status and give me entrance and access to do more with my life. As my eyes looked at the pennies in the pond that day, I resorted to a wish.

In retrospect, my wish was more of a prayer to God. As I uttered the words from my mouth, it was really a plea to God from my heart. I told God that I needed a way out. It wasn't a long wish but it was a heart's cry and God heard. It wasn't long after that I had to leave New Jersey to go live in Brooklyn with my cousin and Mom. My mom who had returned to Jamaica briefly, retired and returned to the United States to be with me. We lived with my cousin for less than a year and secured a furnished room. My mother sacrificed her profession as a senior educator and her comfortable life in Jamaica for my progress and prosperity. She never complained, but I knew she cried. She must have wondered why I wanted to come here to live when I lacked nothing in Jamaica. My dad on the other hand was supportive of the family transition but he always voiced that he would never live in a country to become a second class citizen because he thought people in this country wouldn't accept him as a black man. Our family was a family that did not lack anything. We had our own two story home and car. Both my parents were professionals. My brother and I went to the best schools. We had food, clothes and shelter. What Mom learned years later was it was the dysfunctional and brokenness my heart carried that drove me to run away. I have often said: I came to America and faced hardships. I had a good life in Jamaica. I was actually spoiled. It was here in America that I struggled and faced all types of need. But nothing happens by chance. God had a plan and He wanted me here in America. God has already used me in countless ways and He will continue to expand my territories and use me for His glory. Amen.

Living in New York was a major transition. It was nothing like the quiet and affluent atmosphere of one of the richest towns in New Jersey. Brooklyn was noisy and heavily populated with West Indians then. At that time I had a few friends living in Brooklyn who I knew from Jamaica so we connected. My wish to be married started to manifest through a blind date arranged by one of those friends... Melanie. She was dating an army guy at the time and I was linked with his best friend for a date. His name, Gabriel, a robust Guyanese who stared at me the entire night and I wondered what was his problem and if he had a voice. When I asked why he kept looking at me, he simply smiled and looked away. Anyway, he finally decided to speak and we ended up exchanging numbers to keep in touch because he was also in the army stationed in North Carolina. A very speedy relationship developed between us and Gabriel would leave the army base religiously every two weeks to drive up to visit me. He found out about my situation and at first was apprehensive with continuing the relationship. We loved each other and were two peas in a pod... inseparable. He treated me well, but we were both quite immature. At the time, I worked as a store clerk, earning $200 for 6 days, a hectic 9am to 7pm shift on my feet. It was tiring but God gave me strength. Although I wasn't a heavy church goer, I always prayed. I never doubted that God heard me. God allowed my mother and I the access of jobs that helped with our living arrangements and we were grateful for that furnished room.

My penny in a pond wish continued to manifest when Gabriel decided to ask for help. He drove a GrandAM at the time and would pick me up from the store on his visits. On one of his visits, that Saturday during the day, he came to inform me that two of his car wheels were giving him trouble and so he may not be able to pick me up that night from work because he had no money to replace the wheels. I had just gotten paid and so I went into the changing room, took out $150, gave it to him and told him to get them replaced. He looked at me with a frightful expression when I handed him the money. He resisted, but in my mind and through my voice

I explained to him that he needed to get back to work in North Carolina, so I had to help him. He thanked me, took it, but later returned it. After that incident, not long after, he started talking to me heavily about marriage. I never knew it was a test that caused him to make a decision to marry me. Gabriel had wanted a big wedding, but I was satisfied with a small one and so we agreed to do a bigger wedding as we established ourselves... but it never happened.

My penny pond wish did come true because I got married, had a wonderful son, secured a good job, but that wish started to turn black and blue due to a lie and outside influences that corrupted Gabriel's thoughts against me. My life turned upside down because of one lie. Our marriage started to spiral downwards when my son was born. His army friend who was divorcing his wife due to adultery, lied and told Gabriel that our son was for a different man. Gabriel wasn't open at first with this until years after, but he did show his doubts about our son. The first instance was when my son was born and he asked me at the hospital: "What kind of games are you playing? How is it this child is so light skinned?"

I thought nothing of his remarks and questions because I just had given birth and was excited to hold my son. In retrospect, those were the little signs I missed. One sign I didn't miss however was a dangerous action he committed against our less than a week old son. You see, my son was a colickly baby and would have crying spells at midnight for many hours. Gabriel proved his doubts for our son by tossing our new born in his crib from a distance. I was angry and shocked but that was the day I vowed in my heart I was leaving the marriage. I left the marriage, struggled and sacrificed for my son. Gabriel and I had many face offs over the years and my dear son struggled with rejection until God healed him and showed him that He is His Good Good Father. I too had to come to terms with a broken marriage and surrendered all the issues I faced to God. It was one lie from Gabriel's so called "friend" that spun a marriage into turmoil. Lies are dangerous and this is why God hates lies. It breaks not only hearts, but also families. Lies are destructive and I encourage all who read this: Always tell the truth. Despite how hard it can be to face the truth, always tell the truth. It is better to tell the truth because truth heals and wins even if the truth hurts.

I exited the marriage when my son was less than three years old and my life was ushered into the world of single parenting. Thank goodness to God for my mother who lived with me and my life was much easier than most single mothers. I didn't have the struggle of going to a babysitter or daycare center. I would go to work and school and come home late to a dinner and warm home. I had to pay all the bills and yes it was a struggle but God made a way. Gabriel refused to give child support and he boldly told me to take him to court. I didn't want the hassle but eventually took him to court because when I asked him to pay our son's school fee expenses for private school, he flat out told me: "Your son can go to public school like everybody else." He awakened the beast in me and so I lashed back fiercely. Here I was being nice only asking him to pay for our child's education and I wanted nothing else, not money for food or clothes or medical assistance and his response bit me hard so I went after him fiercely and nastily in return. But God was dealing with me through it all. At the courthouse, the judge was irate when Gabriel complained that he didn't believe our child was his child and so the judge went viciously at him. It seemed as if she took it personally as she spewed insults to his face. She advised him to take a paternity test and literally yelled at him that she was sick and tired of men coming into her courtroom with the same excuses after they had their fun. She calmly called me to her and asked if I wanted retro payments and I told her: "No". She looked at me as if I was crazy, commanded Gabriel to leave the room and asked me if I was sure. I told her "No retro. Let's start from today" She kept reassuring me that it would be a pretty penny because Gabriel was getting paid well, but I didn't care about the money. I cared about the peace. I was losing sleep with all of this hostility between us and I just wanted peace for myself and son. I also wanted my son to have peace and to have a relationship with his father. I also wanted Gabriel to have peace because he had remarried and I learned he had just had a son. I wanted the best for him although he didn't want the same for me. I wasn't going to allow the continuation of black and blue marks to stain my life. I had to change in order to experience change.

My life took several turns while being in America. I call them sudden suddenlies. I know now that God's Hand and His Goodness that never fails has been the constant in my life. He has carved me into His beautiful masterpiece despite the torrid experiences. God has a way of leading us from one level to the next. We may have gotten some punches in life but we must still press on. I was able to gain and learn the lessons. I have learned that God will lead the right people in your life to guide you onward to the other levels of your life. And this is why prayer is extremely important. Learn to lean on God and live a life of prayer. I thought my penny in a pond was a wish, but it was a prayer that shifted my life for the better. It was my faith that the Lord recognized that activated His Hand in my life.

This I know for sure: All things work together for good and God's goodness includes having a prosperous life, being in good health as our lives prosper. I have learned that even if you made a choice that sent your life in a spiral or bizarre direction, God can still use those experiences to glorify His name. There is nothing too hard for God to do. He is able to take us out of the miry clay. In my case, stormy relationships, lies, jealousies, wrong decision and not facing my issues sent my life into insipid seasons, but I eventually always recover from them... thank God. I learned to embrace truth, develop strength, found peace and learned to love and value myself deeply. I have learned that not too many people love themselves and so they struggle to love others properly. We must learn to love God and ourselves deeply. When we do, love ourselves deeply, we establish values worthy to adhere to. We won't allow disrespect or be quick to be disrespectful. When we love ourselves deeply, we will also have the freedom to love others deeply and it is a beautiful place to live lovingly. I have seen the ugliness that comes with hatred and scornful hearts. A scornful hateful heart makes the face of a person's personality look like dirty rags. I encourage you to choose life and choose love. Never let the turmoils of your pastimes make you tense, terrified or tethered. I fought the tentacles of trauma and overcame. I took the time to heal in order to help others heal and now I can say that I am my best terrific and authentic self all because of the Goodness of God!

Epoch 4

Turbulent Turnings

~Tossed into Acknowledging the Truth~

John 8:32 KJV

"And ye shall know the truth and

the truth shall make you free"

One thing I am aware of and love is that the truth sets people free and keep them free. We must endeavour to live a life that exalts truth and speak power to it. This truth telling and truth living begins with ourselves. If we aren't truthful to our own selves, how can we live and be truthful with others? People tend to live a facade about their lives. They put on the best face for the world, and give the worse to those who love them the most. I lived it, so I know it. Some live holiness on Sundays and are the devil's agent the rest of the week or even right after service in the lobby. Let me tell it. Way before my deeper walk of intimacy with God, I surely lived a lie, especially in a marriage that was tormenting the life out of me. I learned that lying to myself was eating away at me slowly and was doing me no good. God had to literally create a crisis in my life where my back was against a wall and my face was towards one door as my option to go through. I had to make a choice whether to escape or to die. I faced the fears and embarrassment and walked through the door to face the truth. The truth was this: My life was a hot mess and I needed help fast. This help was coming from the Lord and He chose the right people to help me. In other words: I had to back it up and surrender fully to God.

The trajectory of my life changed sharply being a single mother balancing motherhood, work and college. It was hard. I wanted so much more for my life and I worked hard and went up the ladder at a banking institution. I gained awards and financial increases. God allowed me to serve managers and supervisors whom He used to favored and promoted me because of my strong work ethics. You see, anything I am assigned to do, I take it seriously and I don't flounce around with my responsibilities. I prospered quickly at the bank, but my interest in college declined. I decided to take one year off that ended up in being out of school for over a decade. As for my spiritual life, I went to church for Christmas and Easter, but I always prayed. One thing I have noticed with being acculturated, if you fail to keep faithful and strong to your roots and faith in God, you can quickly be swept by a system that encourages lusts. That almost happened to me, but God.

When God has a plan for your life, there is an enemy at work designing your downfall. Just as God will use a person for His work on the earth realm, the enemy of God will use another individual for his demonic work on the earth. Think of it like this: You are in the middle of two forces that are at work continually, trying to gain your attention and agreement, to lead you down their path. God wants to lead you on His paths of righteousness and truth, while satan wants to lead you on his path of destruction and lies. And you, being in the middle, have to make the choice which path to take. It is always your choices that will take you to where you are at... whether a blessed place or a cursed position. Learn to choose wisely and learn to make other choices to rise up from the underground lifestyle. Your choice in this life matters.

My path took a turn for the worse when I entered into a relationship with a man I had no business being with. I wasn't taught or warned by my parents about wrong relationships so I was a sheep that entered into a slaughterlike relationship. Of course it did not begin as such. Most relationships start out with sweet talk and lovely treatment, but if you are "woke" there are tell tale signs that will give you alerts that this person is nothing but trouble. I was in a state of lying to myself and suffocating my feelings to please others, hence, I entered the disaster with eyes wide shut. Steph was his name, and he was definitely the worst version of myself. I hadn't given myself enough time to heal from my first failed marriage and here I was bandaging the pain with a man who would have bought me the world if he could. You see, the enemy knew my likes, dislikes and weakness of a kind heart, and so I came into a counterfeit type of kindness that almost destroyed my destiny.

 Steph and I had an extremely stormy relationship for over a decade. We were an "on and off again couple" that argued immensely and passionately over the most insignificant things. Four to five arguments a day would be a good day. A bad day would be over eight arguments that escalated to an apartment that looked shipwrecked. You see, when God isn't in the midst of your life or your relationships, you invite the devil to dilly dally your heart, your time and resources. These turbulent years were the most exhausting and complicated years of my life that if you even suggested that I would get a million dollars for a redo, I would tell you to go fly a kite and get lost. The madness of that relationship broke me down little by little to the point I semi surrendered 80% of my life to God. Semi-surrender you may ask. There is no such thing. Oh yes there is. You can surrender all to God and then you can surrender only portions of you life to Him. I wanted to live for God, but lust still had a hold on me. Let me keep it real for those who can take it real!

In my case, the relationship with Steph was abusive on emotional, physical, spiritual and financial levels. I had a deep relationship with the lust of the eyes and the lusts of the flesh then. Steph bought me nice things and I liked that. The enemy was feeding the cravings of my flesh to the raping and caging of my spirit. This is why you need to be careful who gives you what. It can be an evil exchange to enslave you... to keep you rooted to them. Another issue I battled with was the fear of being alone. Who knows what I am talking about? I had a need to be needed and loved. I wanted attention and in my simpleton thinking, it was better to be in a sad situation that being alone. I was an erroneous optimist, thinking that Steph would change for the best. He didn't... but I did. I got tired of the toxic and caustic words we used towards each other. The recurring malicious behaviors of going to bed vexed in mind and heart wore me down. We broke up and then reignited the flames... of torment! Despite our issues and insane behaviors, I remained faithful to a man I wasn't even married to as yet. I got the strength to walk away from the relationship for a year...... and then we got back together and married.

That year we spent apart, I was able to go to church and I gave my life to God. I accepted Jesus Christ as my Lord and Savior. Giving my life to God was one of the best decisions I have ever made. My relationships changed and I started to go to church more frequently. I steeped myself in prayer and the Bible and my mother thought I was losing my mind. She often worried I was going crazy because she no longer saw her old daughter going to clubs and parties wearing fishnet stockings, pum pum shorts and wearing my hair in different hairstyles each week. She didn't know that the Scriptures say that you become a new creature… old things have passed away, behold the new has come. As I was growing in Christ, the devil was planning my downfall. Through a series of events, Steph and I reconnected and although I thought I was done with him… the devil wasn't done with me.

Steph engaged me for the second time with a bigger ring that had diamonds which you could see from down the block. He knew I converted to Christianity, and so he came to the church, gave his life to Christ he claimed, but his behavior was worse than ever when we married. I went through so much turmoil and torrent throughout the marriage it's a wonder I survived it. I made the tough decision to turn away from a second failed marriage and although I wasn't shattered completely by it... I did fall into a heartset and mindset of not trusting men. To be honest, I am still dealing with trust issues and am asking God to do a complete work with my heart so that I can love again. I am learning that sometimes we have to fail at a thing more than once before we finally get it right and work it right.

In retrospect, Steph and I were both immature and operated in codependency. I, not being healed from the first failed marriage, went into another ill equipped. We must allow the Father to process and heal us COMPLETELY. There are too many wounded people who are wound up in relationships they have no business being in, only to get or give more wounds. If you were to look at their hearts and minds under a spiritual microscope you would see a bevy of spiritual wounds. I was also dealing with the longing of having a father for my son. Gabriel wanted nothing to do with my son, but Steph acted the part as a dad gladly seeing that he had no children and desperately wanted for us to have a child together. The truth was that we both sucked at the marriage. The turbulence I endured over a decade with Steph was grueling but God strategically and lovingly guided me into choosing to turn my life around and surrender more to him. Was it 100 percent surrender?… not yet.

Not only did I overcome a stormy relationship with Steph, my mother and I had our season of tug and war. My mother had identified the danger I was in and sought to warn me in her own way, but in my mind, she was more of an irritant. My dad had to warn her to let me be so I could figure out my life, but he hadn't known that I was being abused. If he had known, Steph would have found himself cut off from the earth at an early age or disabled. My dad knew people that weren't very friendly and all it took was a phone call. I didn't want my dad involved because I thought I was in love. Steph had also played a role in planting seeds of discord between my dearest mom and I because he found we were much too close. I learned that this is what abusers do. They want you away from those who love you and play an instrumental positive role in your life. Abusers don't want their behaviors to be exposed or revealed. They want you to solely be dependent on them and anyone who threatens that dependency, threatens them. The relationship between my Mom and I restored and our bond is stronger than before. The devil lost again. It's amazing how the enemy of your soul and destiny will go to great lengths in a subtle way to consume your life. Like a snake that watches from a distance and slithers its way to you unknowingly, to suddenly strike and inject venom to consume you, this is what your enemies do. This is what Satan does, so be very careful who you link yourself with. Be extremely careful who you marry and who you call friend.

I overcame another failed marriage, but not on my own. God was clearly the One and Only who fought for my life and won the battle. I got the victory because MERCY SAID NO. I had to learn some heavy lessons through it all. I had to learn that I must embrace the truth of what God shows me. I learned to embrace the truth of who people reveal themselves to be. I cannot live a lie and think that lie will somehow disappear. I learned I must not surrender my life into the hands of others for others to control it. I must live my life according to God's plans and let others live theirs. I also learned I shouldn't give people the power over my life, my mind nor my will. God gets that power... not mankind. I learned that what God wants me to know He will send the right people to give me messages, warnings and I must take heed. God told me He loves me and I have value. I am worthy to be loved and cared for and there are those who will love me for me. There are people who may not see your worth or value but know that they are simply blind and that isn't your problem. I had to accept that storms come to wake me up so be aware of what is happening or what's not happening. I learned I must be about my Father's business because I have a purpose so be about His purpose. I needed to grasp tightly that things will change in my life when I changed my mind and actions about certain things. I had to totally depend on and lean on God for sustenance and knowing that being alone and at peace with God is far better than being married and suffering miserably to a beast who is hungry to devour the innocent. God reminded me I lacked nothing but should go to Him first and ask, seek and knock. He gave me the guarantee that surely He would care for me. And finally, God said: Where I lead you, simply follow because the doors I open for you no man can close. He favors me and every place He sends me I have a right to be there. I bring value to the table. How great is our God?

Listen, it is easy to doubt God but we must choose to believe Him because God can be trusted. Let that sink in and say this with me: I BELIEVE GOD. I BELIEVE GOD. I BELIEVE GOD. YES I BELIEVE GOD. When I got out of that horrendous second marriage, I realized I was missing so much in life all because of lies, lusts and fears. I was in a cage that had bars blinding my vision from seeing the full picture. I was so distracted arguing and fighting in a battle that wasn't mine. I found purpose in those years of pain. Those years taught me how to pray and apply faith in God. I am glad though that when the kairos moment came to leave that tossed turbulent life in order to live the truth, I did. Many are still living a tossed turbulent life. Are you one? I am living proof that there is life after two divorces. I have seen people who have been divorced more than twice finally found the love of their life. I believe it will happen for me, but that isn't my main goal. My goals are the goals that God has set for me and I will fulfill them. I thank God for His faithfulness, grace, mercy and love. He kept me safe from the clutches of Satan's destruction and I am grateful He is faithful!

Epoch 5

Forgiven to Forgive

~Progress Comes with Forgiveness~

Matthew 6:14 NIV

*~For if you forgive other people when
they sin against you, your heavenly
Father will also forgive you.~*

So here I was again at ground zero recovering from
another divorce, but this time it was more intense
financially. Despite the hit I endured financially,
this divorce was different. I had peace and relief
that I was out of the turbulence that I weathered
for over a decade.

The recovery process was slow with seasons of crying spells, thoughts of regrets that plagued my mind, shame shadows clouded my vision, disappointments with my life status and boy did the enemy play the blame game with me! God had to take me through the fire, carry me through the mental storms and comforted me through the floods of anguish and pain.

When people say that divorce is hard on a couple and children... believe them! My son was a teen at the time preparing to graduate high school and get ready for college. He did his best to hide his feelings no matter how much I tried to have him share. A mother always knows and feels the pain of her child by looking into their eyes. His pain drove me deeper into prayer for him. He struggled with his classes and his grades plummeted from A's and B's to C's D's. I almost went into crisis mode because I too had returned to college trying to keep it together. I was able to secure the right help to assist him climb and graduate with his Regents diploma. I literally cried when he crossed the stage because he really had to push through to study and pass his exams with all the mental turmoil he endured. I remember when my son made a confession that he had come to his wits end with how Steph was treating me. He was secretly planning to deal with the situation himself. When my son described his intentions I was mortified and I thank God that I came out before it was too late. God knew all along that I had to get out of that turbulence before the beast in my son got out. And this is where I warn you dear sister, for your sake and the sanity of your children, get out of abuse before it is too late. Abuse not only affects you, it deeply affects your children.

When I left Steph, I practically lost most of what I brought to the marriage. When he met me, I was a full woman having my own furniture, money and lifestyle. At the end of the marriage I walked away from 95 percent of my possessions and it broke my heart. I know about loss. I am an expert in loss and at the time it was difficult but God taught me how not to be attached to anything or anyone. Today, I am a woman who isn't excited about a fancy car or posh things anymore. I appreciate them, but I dont idolize them. I believe God slayed the lustful giant in me as I endured loss after loss after loss. I can appreciate nice things and am grateful for them, but I am not tied to anything materialistic anymore.

There was one thing I struggled with that took some time to recover and that was my credit score. I had excellent credit prior to Steph being in my life, but it fell from the upper seven hundreds to lower five hundreds. He left me in much debt that I had to pay on my own. I practically had no money and had to live with a sister in Christ for a month. I later moved and lived with my Pastor and his wife for another month and God blessed me with an apartment in the Heights. I have noticed a trend with God. He places people in our lives at the right time for the right reasons. He uses the people he sends to pour out His love through them unto us. God makes no mistakes and this is why we must be careful how we treat people. You never know who God will use and who is your answer. I am so grateful for all the people who have been a blessing in my life. They have given and shared, loved and listened, fed and allow me to feed, prayed and paid, supported and suffered with me and now I tell you I am grateful for you.

The church I was attending at the time had some awesome leaders. The Bishop and First

Lady helped me tremendously. They made sure to it I was active in ministry. They loved me as their own. They gave of their time and wisdom to lead me in the right direction. I remember a time when Steph somehow discovered the church I attended and visited there. He wanted to reconcile the marriage but I wanted nothing to do with him. There was no going back for me. I was too through and I was repulsed at the thought of even being in the same space with him. I scorned him. I literally hated everything about him. God knew this and was waiting patiently to gain my attention.

When I moved to the Heights, I knew it was God who answered my prayers. He had placed me in the right setting and I lived there for 9 years as I rebuilt my life from the shattered pieces. It happened in a way that only God designed. The rent was what I thought I couldn't afford but

God showed me how and I was never late nor did I struggle to live. Only God! God had me meet and work with my landlady a year before I moved there. That was God's goodness. I lived ten minutes from where I worked and could walk to work during the summers. God's goodness. My son was 20 minutes from school. Who but God? I got a full time position just before I moved there. God again. I always wanted to live on the top floor. God set that up. The window sills were nice and clean.(I have a thing about clean window sills!) God is in the details. Everything was established and designed by God. God answers prayers. I encourage you to rest and rely on God. He is able. He will see you through. Pray and believe God for God can!

The years flew by quickly being at the Heights. I opened up my apartment as a place of refuge for my sister friends to come by and just unwind and relax. If they needed to study... come. I had dinner fellowships and prayer sessions there as well. I celebrated my fortieth birthday there by having a prayer fellowship and the turnout was wonderful. God will surely build and progress your life only if you allow him. But there was one thing that was brewing in me silently that God knew I needed some deep healing. Unforgiveness and bitterness lurked in my heart like a python and I didnt know. The Lord took the opportunity to show me myself and I had to start the process.

Although I was progressing, I still needed more processing. I had unforgiveness lingering in my heart with was affecting my sleep and even my health. I remember having colds and nagging back pains. No matter the physical therapy sessions I took, the pain wouldn't let up. I also noticed that I fell into a mode of not trusting men and I was bitter towards certain types of men that reminded me of Steph. I realized that I was dealing with issues in my tissues with unforgiveness. Steph, Mitch and Gabriel had left bruises in my heart that were festering and not healing. I hadn't given myself permission to heal. I was just band aiding the wounds and adapting to the pain. I hadn't forgiven myself for allowing myself to be treated a certain way by them. I had lots of people to forgive because I wasn't truly free. I had issues in my tissues and those issues were holding me back.

The Lord brought this unforgiveness issue to me early one morning at about three a.m. I used to sleep with gospel music playing and that morning I awoke to a song titled: A Heart that Forgives. Gently and sweetly, the Holy Spirit told me that I needed to forgive and He showed me those whom I needed to forgive. I also needed to reach out to a particular person. He lovingly said: Forgive them. I started to cry and I told God that I had forgiven them. I was being stubborn thinking that I knew more than God. I was in fact lying to myself and to God. I knew the Lord was right and all I needed to do was come into agreement and follow His instructions. This is what I love about the Lord. When we think we know... we really don't know. The heart of God knows what is beating in ours and he knows when the rhythm is off. He sees us for who we are and what we are dealing with. He knows the state of our hearts and knows when it's not in union with His. He identifies with the pain, the residues and issues that are settling in our hearts and he wants us to be cleaned and healed. And so God instructed me what to do and I complied.

You see God wants us to deal with the issues of our past and the issues in our hearts before we can move forward. Its like unpacking luggage from our last trip. There are several dirty clothes in our luggage from our last journey that he wants us to unpack. I don't know about you, but when I get back from my vacation, I unpack my suitcase the following day. I want the "dirties" out and have my suitcase ready and available for my next trip. It is only a crazy person who will take dirty clothes already existing in a suitcase to another trip. God wants us to unpack the unforgiveness, the bitterness, the lies, the disorder, the dramas, the pain, and all the "dirties" before we can go to the next level. If your heart's too heavy with issues in the tissues, then you're not ready for His blessed best. In this journey called life, we will experience many things, but if we are too encumbered with issues of the past then we aren't light enough to fly high and soar to new exciting levels. God wanted me to forgive and move forward and so I had to face my fears. Truly there is progress with forgiveness.

We are to have a heart that forgives. God doesn't want us to have a broken heart or to manage living while tolerating pain. Unforgiveness breeds bitterness and will affect your health as it once upon a time did mine. When I forgave and released the people who made me bitter, my back pain slowly went away. Today I can say I am pain free and I know it's because I no longer have issues of unforgiveness. God wants us free.

I pray that you will pray and ask the Lord to show you your spiritual heart. It is possible that your heart has some unresolved issues stacked in the crevices and corners. Allow God access to touch, heal and deliver you from those issues for only He can. What I know for sure is this: The beauty of God's goodness includes giving us the strength to forgive others, to forgive ourselves and to receive God's forgiveness when we fall short.

Epoch 6

Unafraid of Fear

~No Longer a Slave to Fear~

2 Timothy 1:7 NKJV

"For God has not given us the spirit of fear, but of power and of love and of a sound mind"

I am ever so grateful for this Scripture that is a strong reminder of what God gives us compared to what He hasn't given us. God gives us the Spirit of POWER, LOVE and a sound mind. God does not and has no part with giving us fear. God does not impart fear in us. God will not feed us fear. Get that today. Thank Him for what He has given us….. **love, power and a sound mind.**

God, I thank you for the Spirit of power, of love and of a sound mind. Thank you for giving these to me.

For too many years, I battled with all types of fears. Those fears were a mixture of different things such as rejection, low self esteem, insecurities, failures, loving myself totally and being my authentic self. Those years I was a totally different person compared to now. I would suffocate my voice to please others because I thought what I had to say wasn't relevant until I heard people say exactly what was in my head. Satan sought to block my progress and sabotage my thinking until the Lord had to show me how to overcome.

Being married to Steph was definitely my biggest test to overcome my fears. He being an abuser thought he would have the final say over my life. I proved wrong those spirits of fear, terror and error. Although the negative words that were spoken to me by him were meant to discourage me to lose hope, I rose up above them and hope was strengthened. I think back and smile because my name is a testament of who I am. My hope in God was tested and God allowed me to learn that I must continually put my hope in Him for I will not be brought to shame. Hope has solidified in me that now I am able to empower the hopeless by showing them to place their hope fully in the Lord.

Isaiah 49:23d NIV states, "... those who put their hope in me will not be put to shame."

One thing I would like to share about fear is this: *Fear lies to you boldly in an attempt for you to believe it's the truth. Fear also threatens you from moving forward from your comfort level. Fear makes you question yourself. Fear*

shouts to your mind with more intensity once you give it attention.

You will hear words like:

"You can't"

"You aren't enough"

"You don't have what it takes"

"Leave"

"Run"

"Quit"

"You'll make a fool of yourself"

"People won't care or believe"

"No"

"You will fail"

Have you ever heard God speaking like this to anyone in the Bible? So where are these negative words coming from? Those words are words of fear and God DOES NOT GIVE US A SPIRIT OF FEAR!!!!!!

I have also learned that fear will revisit you often to retest if you have really overcome. Who will agree with me on this? Yes, fear doesn't give up easily and neither should you give in easily BUT FIGHT TO THE FINISH!

I remember when I had first left Steph and he was insistent to recalibrate the marriage. He used tears of pity, then got hostile again. All this was happening via the phone. When he realized that I wasn't budging he started to mildly threaten me with scenarios. He asked me questions and used statements like:

"How will you manage?" "Nobody will want you." "You will come running back."

All he was doing was chasing me further away because I was mentally done and my heart had packed up and left permanently. I remember when the Holy Spirit instructed me to change my telephone number. I was a bit apprehensive at first, for we had joint financial responsibilities and I wanted to make sure he paid on time, but I knew I had to listen to God. When God speaks to us, we should not delay. He knows all the components of why He wants us to do what we need to do. We don't need to know everything. All we need to do is obey instructions because oftentimes obedience is for our protection. The day I finally decided to change the number was because we had gotten into a huge argument over a bill. That was the moment God told me to hang up the phone and change the number. When I did so, I recovered my peace. There are times we have to go to great lengths to guard our peace, guard our minds and protect our future. Sometimes we need to shut out and resist those who claim we are the problem. If you are always the problem then rid yourself of the complainers. We cannot resort to fear because of our reasonings or what others try to project on us. God is above our reasonings of how things will manifest. We need to believe God and use our power of obedience, as well as, doing all we need to in order to combat and overcome fear.

Fear desires to zap our strength and make our hearts feel like a failure, but God wants us to know that we have Him as our constant whom we can trust. When we keep in our mind that God is our all in all, then we will not be disappointed. Despite outcomes in our lives, know for sure that God knows best and He works everything out best. Our lives may shift... people may disappoint us... but God is our strength and our portion forever.

Psalm 73 vs. 26 KJV states:

"My flesh and my heart faileth: but God is the strength of my heart, and my portion forever."

One day I had a transformative conversation with my coworker about the topic of fear. I simply asked her about her perspective of fear. This was her timely and wise response:

"Fear tests you. It tests the true fabric within you. It makes you see yourself. Fear wants to know if you can withstand the heat. Fear comes to determine what fabric you are made of. Are you cotton, silk, rayon or polyester?"

Wow. I was taken to a higher height after hearing her perspective of fear because it's laden with truth.

My question for us is: "If fear is imagined fire, do we melt easily by its imagined heat?"

Dealing with fear can be frustrating but we must be stronger than it. God will also put us in arenas where we will have to overcome fear. I remember when I had to start teaching and do my prayer sessions on the radio. I had no clue what to do and wanted to back out but I pressed through. God proved to me that I had to get out of my comfort zone and get into the territories that I needed to be in order to show forth His power and glory!

I am learning daily that God doesn't want any of His children stuck in situations that are below His standards. When it is time for us to move, God will show us how and when. We are to be leveling up in faith often and this means we have to take back some territories that fear is occupying illegally. God wants His business accomplished and He needs us to work through.

Another testimony of overcoming fear happened in 2004. My life drastically went into a different direction that year. I had worked in corporate America at a well known bank for about a decade. I rose up the corporate ladder quickly because God favored me and I learned quickly.

Then, God started to shake my comfortable work nest and I surely didn't like it. The Holy Spirit informed me that it was time to wrap up this season of my life. It was time to leave banking and I literally froze when I heard that. I was making good money and there was no reason I could give to leave, but God kept speaking. I tried everything to tune Him out because of fear, but no one can tune God out for long. You see, when fear grips you, you want to hide in the bushes and camouflage as a twig, but God won't have it. He will find you in the bushes and become a thorn to drive you out. You see, when God has a call on your life, you either obey or deal with the consequences of disobedience. I toggled between two decisions of staying in corporate or obeying the leadership of the Holy Spirit. I couldn't ignore the voice of the Lord any longer and then what happened next was God started to shake my nest on the job much harder. The heat was on. I eventually conquered my fear of the unknown future and took that leap of faith and left my job. It wasn't the easiest decision or transition to walk away from security to the unknown, but God surely provided well and good for us.

I have realized that we cannot be afraid of what God instructs us to do. It's all designed by Him on purpose. We must ensure that it is the voice of the Lord we have heard and simply obey. I have come to find that our lives are planned on purpose for His divine purposes. We are not random beings living a random life. There are different seasons that we will face and we need to make different decisions and those decisions may invoke those insecurities, fears and issues that are hidden within us, but God wants us to overcome them, step up and be bold to confront every monster or beast of fear that seek to limit us. We are to be courageous and be strong in the Lord and in the power of His might. We are to say "no" to fears. We are to speak up, look up and walk into our destined places that God has prepared for us.

Finally, know that the fears in others will come straight into your presence facing you. This could happen anywhere and through anyone. Wherever you interact with people who are carriers of insecurities and fears, whether it be on your job, at church, at the mall, a family barbeque, in a meeting board room etc. these fear carriers are coming and you must be prepared. Some people are known to project their insecurities and fears on others especially if they sense, think or perceive you are weak and fearful. I have come across people who deliberately tried to test my character because I carry a sweet and pleasant demeanor. It is only when they crossed the line they realize that my sweetness shouldn't be mistaken for weakness.

I have discovered over the years being in different churches, that there are bullies and hypocritical characters in the church. Did I hear an Amen? Yes. There are bullies in the church and many of them are in leadership thinking that their titles frighten others. **There is one thing I learned fast: It's not a title that makes a person reputable. Its their ability to manage power and authority.**

A person can have a million titles and positions of prestige, but if the spirit of God is not at work in and through them, then their titles and positions are useless and a sham.

The Lord had to personally teach me not to fight battles at the same level the battles were created or occur. This means: You have to climb higher with different weapons to beat the enemy and his schemes and tactics.

As Michelle Obama has frequently stated: "When they go low... you go high"

When battles come and the enemy is wielding an ax to drive you out of the land, kneel and pray. Fast and pray. Praise and worship. Decree and declare the word of God and keep humble. People who are ill mannered and ill tempered, even in the church, will try to get at you but know who you serve and who sent you. He is already fighting for your cause. Where God places us, He protects us. Where God sends us, our Savior is with us. He will never leave us nor forsake us so there is nothing or none to fear.

I am no longer a slave to fear. I am an anointed child of God filled with faith, power, love and a sound mind. Amen!

Epoch 7

Prepared Through Patience and Peace

~Teaching and Teachable Moments~

Isaiah 26:3 KJV

"Thou wilt keep him in perfect

peace, whose mind is stayed on thee;

because he trusteth in thee"

Life is truly an interesting undulating journey filled with different seasons where you will have an elixir of laughter, tears, painful memories and more. It is up to us how we respond to what is happening around us, in us and to us. We can either become better, bitter, keep being bitten or bite our way through. We simply have to keep learning instead of burning. The more we learn, the more we know and the more we grow.

The different seasons I have gone through have allowed me to gain much wisdom and insight to the point I can help others. I have learned to roll with the punches and keep smiling. I have gotten to a point where I have enough tolerance to ignore a lot of the bull nonsense that comes my way. I can see a joker coming from a mile. I can see a player through a smile. I can discern a fake hug and a lustful gleam in the eye. I know when people are carding the psychological tactics and as for the liars and haters, they ooze from their pores visible notes that play in the air, an out of date tune. To be honest, sometimes I play along to see how far people will play their game and then when I think I have learned enough, I withdraw. Listen, when people play with you, sometimes you have to play the game as well, because it can be used as a teachable moment to wisen up. But, I wasn't always like this. I had to learn the hard way. At times when you love hard and strong the wrong ones, you get hurt the same.

One thing I know for sure and its this: ***What doesn't break you, makes you a whole lot stronger. I also know that nothing occurs randomly in our lives. There are lessons that we must learn in order to operate efficiently in certain settings. We can either fight the lessons we need to learn or choose to learn from them.*** Here is some advice that I believe you can use: Always ask yourself **WHY?** Why am I here? Why am I doing what I am doing? Why is this in my presence? Why am I upset? Why do I feel like this? Don't be afraid to ask yourself WHY? Give yourself permission to ask yourself WHY? Then attempt to answer the WHY? You will find some clarity that will either shift you in another direction or strengthen your choice so that you can gain peace. Some why's you may never get an answer and this is where you simply depend on God and accept what He has sent for you to endure.

Once upon a time I lacked patience and peace. These twins were characteristics I needed to develop. Throughout my early teens into my twenties and thirties, I was quite an impatient person. That struggle with impatience would affect my peace and I was certainly a lighted firecracker on a roller coaster ride. I wanted things to happen in my own timing and if it didn't, I went into fireworks mode and believe me it wasn't pretty. But God had a different agenda on how to deal with all that fireworks in me. I had to be tamed and so I was led into different arenas that calmed those fireworks down. God now uses the fireworks in me for His glory.

God worked strategically in my life to help me grow and develop in these two areas. He did so by purging my life of incorrect relationships, shaped my thoughts that affected my actions, strengthened my heart from intentional attacks and so much more. Pray and ask God to help you and He will. He can purge you, strengthen you and guard you but you need to ask Him to. In doing so, I believe that God will work a good work in you and through you Amen. I have become a much stronger woman because I allowed God to work on me. I am less emotional and impulsive with my responses to situations. I don't react anymore about what I face, but I pause, think, process and invite the Holy Spirit to reveal to me what I need to know and to do. I am no longer a cry baby being offended or annoyed by the behaviors, words and mentalities of others. Once upon a time I used to pine for days and months over what was done or said to me. Presently, I look at or listen to the bull nonsense for a hot second, deal with it and move on. I learnt over the years that getting heated and having temper tantrums were not the answers and so I had to develop self control. The Lord showed me how to pray, trust Him, rest in His Word, obey His Word, follow His leadership, praise my way through and He would work it out for my good.

My biggest test with patience and peace was one that God designed and assigned that made me experience a significant growth spurt. I was assigned a student who was not so patient himself. He wanted what he wanted quickly and if his demands were not given immediately, he would yell, scream, shout and put on such a production it left me in awe. As I write this, I wonder if this is how God saw me behaving in the Spirit realm when I became impatient. I am truly amazed how God will have us come face to face with an extreme version of our inner issues so we can see ourselves for ourself. So this student was only 5 years old but he was a genius. He knew exactly what to do to push my buttons and I knew that God was using this little one to encourage me to come up higher. I received my training and grew to love this little one who not only changed for the better, but I too changed for the better.

My experience with this little one taught me so much about myself and my own behaviors, my likes and dislikes. Although at first he wouldn't obey my orders, I realized it wasn't my orders were the problem. It was my delivery. It was my tone. I had to alter the way I spoke and restructure my delivery. My mother always said: "You will always catch more flies with something sweet."

This is not to attribute a fly with a child. My point is: I had to be more sweeter in Spirit, heart and mannerisms in order to get people to do things you propose to them. No one wants to drink vinegar, so give them honey. But I also learned that manipulative people will try to take your sweetness for weakness so I had to be mindful of the snakes as well. Working with this little one also showed me how to be mindful of my frustration levels. I learned that if I allowed this child's behavior to get me frustrated, annoyed, ticked off, overwhelmed and erratic for simple things, then I needed to see that I was immature and needed to grow up. I had to put things into perspective. This child was a child. I have the tools to use to help him, so help him. If I didn't have the tools, ask for the tools. If I still needed to acquire more tools, I simply needed to find the tools somehow somewhere. I needed to find what worked and work it! And so I did and this strategy made my life and his life easier throughout the school year. Most of all, I learned I had to work temperance and love into his world because he had many changes and challenges occurring in his life. Sometimes all we need to give others is love from the heart, rather than knowledge from the head.

I also learned that **I AM NOT IN CONTROL!** Can you say that out loud about two more times? There are many things we are simply not in control of and we just have to eat that apple and swallow it. Too often we want to be in control of everything and life isn't a cookie cutter. We must learn to release control and tap into what the Father wants and how the Father wants us to handle situations. Throughout the year, God taught me strategies of how to rest in Him. He wanted me to lean on Him fully. The days when the little one was "turned up" having meltdowns that made me slide all day, I had to just whisper a prayer and ask God for strength to remain peaceful and patient as the storm passed by. I was able to apply this strategy in my own personal life to those storms that came. I had to rest in His arms and whisper a prayer…. "Lord give me the strength, courage, peace and patience as the storm passes by." And the storm passed by and I survived and came out better with peace and patience on the other side.

This assignment with the little one really branded and molded me for life. I am grateful that God saw that I needed this training and trusted me with this child. When others laughed at me as I struggled with him in the beginning, I stood the course with him and out this little one came out victoriously. All glory to God for what He has done!

God will choose you! Can you say that again? There are some assignments that have your name on it, because only you have the anointing to handle those assignments. God knows the oil and the gift He placed inside you. My mother has taught me never to chase after anything or anyone. What is meant for you, is yours and it will find its way to you at the right time. Who is appointed to you, will make their way to you. Like Jesus, the people who needed Him, found their way to Him. ***To Him. To Him.*** There are those who are assigned ***to you*** and you have to give them what they have come for. God's gift. The oil. There are some people who are educated for a job while there are others who are simply skilled, gifted and anointed to do the same job. A gift from God isn't bought. Rather, it's a blessing. Where one has to study for decades, the gifted simply does what they are created to do. I believe that God activated the gift He placed inside me to work in this little child's life. God also used this activation to prune me to be more patient and peaceful having reliance on Him. In addition, it was surely a preparation to do more ministry for His glory.

Having peace and learning to practice patience is a beautiful place to be spiritually. God wants us to be stable in him. God wants us to be anchored in Him. We need to learn to be patient with God, ourselves and others. We need to have the peace of God as our fulcrum and within our very membranes of our beings. We need this peace in order to operate even in the midst of the storms of life, just as Jesus was, as He slept through it with the disciples in the boat, because He is the Master over every storm.

Epoch 8

Gracefully Broken

~Ordained and Ordered to God~

Matthew 28 vs. 19-20 NIV

"Go therefore and make disciples of all the
nations, baptizing them in the name of the
Father and of the Son and of the Holy Spirit,
teaching them to observe all things that I
have commanded you; and lo, I am with
you always, even to the end of the age."

As you can tell, my life has been a bitter sweet
concoction of joys and sadness but it was all for
God's glory. These myriad of experiences often

held times where my heart was broken repeatedly. I was gracefully broken and I can now say that it was good that I was afflicted. The afflictions made me stronger and wiser and now I am thankful. Why so? I am more equipped to help others and I have a heart for the broken.

Ministry is hard work. Let me repeat. Ministry is hard work and you will often go through brokenness and pain in order to sympathize with those who are broken. You will face mockery in the spirit, spat on by toxic people, snarled at by jealous folks, lied on by the petty and stand alone against the masses. Jesus is our typical example of the abuses He endured such as: scorn, hatred, heartbreak, pain, and so much more. If Jesus dealt with that my friend, in ministry, you will too. It's not an easy road.

Through it all, the process has built in me a resilience like no other where I can serve God's people with love and intentionality despite what's going on in my personal life. I believe that every tear I shed became a protective shield around my heart. I know that every heartbreak and rejection I faced created a fountain of love for others. For every encounter of jealousy, envy, strife and spite against me that battled my mind, those became a crown of wisdom and that wisdom is now a library I refer back to often.

When I speak to my dear Mom, who is 85 years at the time of this writing, she often tells me that I am a strong woman. I smile at this because I admire her strength of how she overcame poverty, jealousy, disease and trauma. She however believes that my depth of strength is at an exponential level to hers. I watched my mother at a tender age study and pushed through some mighty hurdles that came her way. Her strength in me has always been at work ever since

I was a little girl. As early as five years old, I knew I was different from other children. Being the youngest and only daughter for my parents, I was quite sheltered. I never had lots of friends growing up and although I know many people now, my closest friends are a chosen few. I never liked crowds, noise, cursing, and loud music but I learned to tolerate certain scenarios temporarily. One thing I have always been sensitive to and that is the needs of the hurting. I could see the pain of others in their eyes, voice, countenance and gait.

One of my brother in Christ Levy, told me one day: "Sis, you have a Pastor's heart."

His words struck a confirming chord because an eight year old student wrote a poem for me in 2013 and she stated the same thing. To this day, I have that poem in my bedroom. I know that God will continue to use my heart of compassion to help those who need love and hope. Although

I have a heart of compassion, I am allergic to foolishness. I am repulsed when I see injustice and when people deliberately put into practice behaviours that are detrimental to their lives. I take the call of God seriously and God wants us to live a life of holiness and truth, not hypocrisy and lies. One thing I have witnessed over and over and it's this:People play games with their soul salvation. This includes ministry leaders who entertain and wrap themselves in the lusts of the eyes, the lusts of the flesh and the pride of life. And when they wrap themselves with these, then they end up warping their lives. I know, because my life almost got trapped in that type of living. I had to repent and ask God to save me and keep me from deception.

Once upon a time I was so wrapped in lusts it warped my life. I mistakenly thought that lust was love. I thought that sex was the answer that made husbands and men happy and they wouldn't leave. I thought having the next dress or shoes or jewelry would make me happy. God had to teach me that true joy and fulfillment came from Him. He is my joy. He is my One True Love. He fills me. Whatever I need I can run to Him.

I must tell you this and you can choose to believe it: Anything done outside of the context of what God ordains is calling for nothing but drama and trouble. Sex before marriage is not ordained by God and it is titled as **SIN.** Adultery is SIN. There are many sexual sins that people tend to excuse and will casually state: *"God will forgive."* Yes God forgives sin, but if we know to do good and not do it then it is sin. Why would a sane individual who is bleeding want to jump into a shark infested ocean to take a swim? That individual will be circled in no time and devoured. That is what sin does... devours you eventually. It you go swimming in shark tanks bleeding you then become shreds! The lust of the flesh is a difficult struggle and it is a bondage that refuses to let go. You have to do your part and ask God to clean you, keep you, and show you the way. If God did it for me through fasting, praying, feeding on the Word of God, praising, being mindful of my surroundings and who I entertain, then His hands will move on your behalf. You will be gracefully broken!!

God does everything in order so that when it's time to be used by Him, then you have been prepared suitably to represent Him. Some people choose to go through the process of preparation to be sent, but others forfeit the process and send themselves. Never send yourself. It is better when God anoints and appoints you. I have sat in pews and witnessed how some in leadership treat the flock with contempt because they think they have a higher position. Some leaders lack humility and love. Some leaders show one face on Sunday, but a hell raiser on Wednesdays or in the bathroom after Sunday service. Oh, let me tell it! They use their leadership position as a ticket for undercover abuse. What they fail to realize is that God is taking log of it all.

The bible says in Hebrews 10:31 KJV:

"It is a terrible thing to fall in the Hands of the living Lord."

Too many ministers, evangelists, teachers, preachers, prophets, bishops, etc are not reverencing God and the call. Holy standards are being shoved under the carpet. Some churches are filled with spiritual garbage and God isn't blind to it. Profit takes the place of the prophet to speak out and warn the people of their ways in the church. God isn't asleep and will have the last say on the last day. It is time to be right, not get right. Tomorrow isn't promised to anyone.

I have served in different ministries at different churches and I have seen and experienced much. Some were pleasant experiences and some absolutely not. One thing that remains true and its this: The truth eventually reveals itself about the nature of those in the church. We shouldn't judge or look down on others, but to pray for them. I too was straddling the fence until God had to "fix my business". I had to learn that I couldn't live the way I wanted and be a Christian. My life was to be different from the rest and so I had to "come ye out from amongst them" When I did, God did a mighty work in me in preparation to ordain me as a Chaplain.

God used Dr. B as the vessel to ordain me on April 27th 2019. I met Dr. B at the radio studio I ministered the gospel. God used my brother to speak to me prophetically. He said to go on radio. At first I didn't believe I could do radio, but I went forward on the instructions. God connected me with others who led me in the right direction. I excelled at radio and am so grateful that my brother was obedient to speak what the Lord instructed. It was at the radio station I met Dr. B who encouraged me and helped me with such passion. I admire him so much and thank God for his heart and passion for people from all walks of life. In a series of events, he invited me to a chaplain ordination and the power of God came upon me. What Dr. B didn't know was that God had been speaking to me about chaplaincy the year before, but I had filed it to the side. Then the Lord reminded me of what He had told me to research chaplaincy. That's when the Spirit of the Lord intervened and showed me the connection. Dr. B was who God chose to ordain me as a chaplain and I am grateful. God gave Dr. B the eyes to see His work and anointing upon me and he did what God assigned just for him to do. What God does, no one should question. Amen.

The day before my ordination I spent time in prayer, fasting, worship and the word. I remember listening to a song that broke me down into tears. I cried from the bowels of my soul. The Lord took me on a flashback landscape of the different seasons I endured and overcame. The Lord spoke to my heart and said: "You had to go through all of that to get to this place. I am sending you to go and do my work for my glory." I felt the Presence of God rain upon me in the room and it was absolutely beautiful.

The day of the ordination was powerful and set by the hand of God. God spoke through Apostle L. His messages have been manifesting. He also warned me of what was to come and how to handle them. God is thorough in what He does and all we have to do is follow His leading. God will lead us. We simply need to follow Him. O how faithful is our God who is mighty in what He does and says!

I have been gracefully broken, ordained and ordered to Go! I know that none can stop the call of God on my life. The only person who can stop me is me and **I WILL NOT STOP! I GO AS GOD SAYS BECAUSE GOD HAS CALLED ME AND I SHALL NOT STOP FROM DOING WHAT GOD HAS CALLED ME TO DO IN JESUS NAME AMEN!**

I am no different from you. I am a person with a purpose who has simply surrendered to God. This is what life is all about when it comes to God... ***SURRENDER***! Too many people refuse to surrender because they want to do life their way and not God's way. The difference is clear when we give the reins of life to God. Hear this: No matter what you have done or gone through, or what you think you have or don't have, God can use you if you allow Him to. God is with you. He is Emmanuel, God with us. He came to save us but also to be with us and live in us through the power of the Holy Spirit. We are never alone. He will work things out for us. We need to understand that our lives have been planned way before we were born so its best to stick with God and find out what God has lined up next for us to do and ask Him for guidance to do it. In doing what God wants, it will be well with our souls.

God provides for what He wants us to produce. Believe that. He also protects us and prospers the works of our hands for it is His Hands at work through us Amen? He did it for me and He will do it for you too. Take up your cross and follow the Lord. Surrender it all to Him. May it be well with your soul! Amen!

A final note: Are you saved? Have you been encouraged by my life story? Do you want to experience the Hand of the Living God in your life? It takes a decision to believe that God loves you. He sent His only son to save you from destruction in this life and the life to come. Will you say yes to Jesus today? If yes, then pray this prayer with me: Father, I believe you have a purpose and plan for my life. Do a new work in my life. I want you to show me the way. Forgive me of my stubborn ways. Forgive me of all my sins. Come into my heart and live. Use me for your glory today and always in Jesus name Amen!

Psalm 23:6 NIV

"Surely goodness and mercy shall follow me all the days of my life; and I will dwell in the house of the Lord forever."

Printed in the United States
By Bookmasters